Contents

2000 years since what...?

The Dome!

The biggest party ever!

Millennium bugs!

Why all the fuss about the beginning of the year 2000? Is it all an excuse for television presenters and the tourist industry to go mad? Won't your life be exactly the same on 1 January 2000 as it was on 31 December 1999?

Yes, it will, unless the rumours are right about the bug, traffic lights being out of time, cars not starting, aeroplanes being grounded, etc. But apart from that...

It's easy to forget the real reason why there is anything to celebrate at all. So this book begins with the past, with lots of information about Jesus, whose birth two thousand years ago (or thereabouts) is the real reason for the party. In the present, there are extracts of stories people read today, which have been influenced by the life of Jesus. And then we've asked lots of people to look to the future, to tell us what present they would give to a child born on 1 January 2000.

We hope you enjoy reading *Stories for the Millennium*. Keep it as your Millennium souvenir!

Have a great future!

Stories for the Millennium

A special book to celebrate the Millennium

Scripture Union,
207-209 Queensway,
Bletchley,
MK2 2EB,
England.
© Scripture Union 1999, Reprinted 1999 twice.

With special thanks to the churches in Plymouth for the bright idea which gave birth to this book. And to the Drummond Trust, 3 Pitt Terrace, Stirling, for their generosity.

ISBN 1 85999 331 1

British Library Cataloguing-in-Publication Data
A catalogue record for this book is available from the British Library.

Cover design by David Lund Design
Designed by Grax Design

Printed and bound in Great Britain by Ebenezer Baylis and Son Ltd, The Trinity Press, Worcester and London

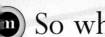 # So what is the Millennium?

The Millennium is a great opportunity to mark the passing of time. But that's not the whole point of it....

What do people still remember about Jesus from 2000 years ago?

- A man who has had more impact on history than any other individual.
- The things he did, which have been learned and copied for 2000 years.
- The things he said, which have been studied and understood for 2000 years. The amazing story of Jesus coming alive after being put to death on a cross. The fact that Jesus said he will always be with all people for all time.

What happened in 1 AD?

- Jesus may have been born. (More likely, he was born four or five years earlier.)
- Other people were born, others died.
- Wars were fought and peace was found. (Julius Caesar had come and gone in the British Isles. He didn't like the weather!)
- The Celts had also invaded the British Isles...and they stayed.
- The Romans ruled Israel. They held a population count. Everyone who lived in the Roman Empire had to take part. That included Israel.

So people remember Jesus. The Millennium is about his 2000th birthday. Read on to find out how it all started...

Dear Friends,

It's been such a hard and strange year for us. First of all we (that's my wife Mary, and I) were both visited by an angel. That shook us up, I can tell you. The angel told us we'd have a child who would be a boy. We were even given his name - Jesus! Then, even though Mary was pregnant and pretty large, we travelled to Bethlehem for the census. That's because the Romans were collecting everyone's name. We couldn't find anywhere to sleep. We ended up staying in a cold, dirty and smelly animal shed.

Late one night, our son was born. We were startled when a crowd of shepherds just turned up. They'd heard about our son, Jesus, so left their sheep and came to worship him. Then a bit later, along came some wise men. They had travelled a great distance and brought very expensive gifts.

Jesus was a few months old when we had to escape to Egypt (a long, long, way away). We went just in time because the army began to kill newborn boys around Bethlehem. Mary and I have thought a lot about our son - we believe God has shown us he is going to be someone special.

Thanks for your friendship,

Mary and Joseph (and baby Jesus)

esus.homelife/webpage@theMillennium

Family
- the son of Mary and Joseph; has a well-known cousin, a few months older than he is, called John the Baptist.

Early years
- normal childhood; father a carpenter in small town of Nazareth; probably helped father in workshop; went to the village synagogue school and learned the teachings in the Jewish writings.

Young teen
- aged twelve, got lost when in Jerusalem (over 100km from home) for the big annual festival of Passover; parents eventually found him learning from and talking to the wise religious teachers at the temple!

✗ Travelling
- around age of 30 started his work of healing and speaking to people about God; travelled from place to place; from that time on, didn't really have a home base, but stayed with friends in the towns and villages he visited.

✓ Favourite stays
- staying with the sisters, Mary and Martha, in the village of Bethany.
- stopped off for a meal in Jericho, with a cheating tax collector called Zacchaeus.

✗ Scary stays
- didn't like to go back to his hometown, Nazareth, because some people there didn't understand Jesus and threatened to push him over a hillside ledge;
- near the end of his life, was thrown into prison.

What did Jesus do that caused such a fuss? Here's a report on his early life. (Jesus would have gone to school at the local synagogue but he wouldn't have had a report quite like this!)

Report

Name: Jesus of Nazareth　　　　　　**Date: 32 AD**

Geography

Good knowledge of roads in the area as he walks long distances between towns and villages. Knows about water transport too as he sometimes sails on Lake Galilee.

History

Great interest in the Jewish religious writings and knows all about leaders from the past, such as Abraham, David and Moses. He uses this knowledge to teach others how God wants people to live.

Religious Education

There's never been anyone better at this subject! He has serious discussions with senior religious leaders.

Science

Clearly understands how the world works. He knows how to repair sick and unhappy people. He is able to stop storms on Lake Galilee and he can even walk on water!

Social development

Jesus is good at getting along with people, although some are puzzled by him. Not everyone likes him. He has healed people who couldn't walk, those who couldn't see and who had awful skin diseases. He has also brought three people back to life, who had been pronounced dead.

Comment

Jesus is an outstanding person who changes lives wherever he goes. Jesus of Nazareth has a bright future ahead of him and will bring light to the world.

m What's in a name?

Jesus of Nazareth was only one of the names or titles of the man whose birth we are celebrating in the year 2000.

Jesus

or Joshua, a common name, meaning 'one who saves'.

JESUS OF NAZARETH

'...of Nazareth' was often added to identify him from others also called 'Jesus' who lived elsewhere. Jesus was brought up in Nazareth.

Jesus bar Joseph

'bar' means 'son of', so Jesus bar Joseph means 'Jesus, son of Joseph'.

Teacher

People often called him 'Teacher'. They had a lot of respect for his teaching. Jesus taught about God and how God wants us to live. He was a great storyteller.

Messiah/Christ

'Messiah' is a Hebrew word and 'Christ' is Greek, meaning 'the anointed one' or the person who has been chosen for a special task, like a king. People in the time of Jesus were expecting a king to be born who would do great things. Jesus was seen by some as this promised leader.

The longer Jesus was around, more people realised that, in some ways, he was no ordinary man. Some understood that God had sent his Son, Jesus, to the earth. Many said that the fact that Jesus came alive again was proof that he was God.

Son of God

STOP PRESS !

 Jesus had his enemies.
They made him suffer.

JESUS ARRESTED AND QUESTIONED

The chief priests, worried about the popularity of Jesus, have arrested him. These religious leaders accuse him of insulting God. But his friends say Jesus is the Son of God. There are rumours he may be sentenced to death.

JESUS DIES, SKY GOES BLACK

The shock decision to crucify Jesus, along with two common thieves, was carried out today. Jesus was nailed to a cross and finally died. The sky was black he died. Soldiers stabbed his s with a sword to make sure he really was dead. His body is to removed and taken to a tomb into the hillside.

JESUS NOT DEAD, FRIENDS DELIGHTED

The friends of Jesus, the man who was crucified three days ago, have made an extraordinary claim. They say that Jesus, who was certainly dead, is now alive again. Some people say they have even seen him and heard him speak. Others say angels told them what had happened. The chief priests, who are now very worried, refuse to comment.

JESUS VANISHES TO HEAVEN

It is reported that Jesus, who has been see alive by over 500 people, has gone to heav Before he vanished into a cloud, he spoke his followers. He promised them the powe to tell others about God. Already groups his followers are planning to meet and pra together.

ⓜ Story times

Imagine a really good story: a great opening gets you interested. Plenty of mystery or excitement keeps you turning the pages right to the end. At last, you know what's happened. The end. What a let-down! It's finished, all over.

But the story of Jesus didn't finish when he went back to heaven. Quite the opposite. The followers of Jesus have a story that's already lasted 2000 years, and the story still goes on.

It began just after Jesus came alive again and the lights went on in the minds of his followers. Then the story went through awful times when to be known as a Christian could mean death by beating, hanging or, in Roman times, becoming lunch for the lions! (Since Jesus came alive again, Christians believe that death is not the end of everything.)

But the story has seen good times too. Hundreds and thousands of people have realised that Jesus can be with them too, to help make sense of their lives. Battles have been fought in the name of Christianity. Christians have disagreed over what are the right and the wrong things to believe. Yet the Christian faith has grown, spread over the whole world and is still spreading today. To find out how, read on!

It's great to be in teams, clubs, groups and gangs. What groups are you in? Guides? Scouts? Football team? The How-to-miss-PE club? One thing's for sure - you wouldn't bother getting together with others unless you thought it was worth it.

Crowding into a little room were the first believers in Jesus. They had seen Jesus after he'd come alive again. They'd seen him vanish into heaven. As they sat together, they planned what they would do and asked God to help them. Suddenly, something like flames landed on their heads. At that moment they received the power from God they needed and they set out to tell others.

Paul who was the first great Christian preacher, wasn't one of those first believers. In fact, he thought followers of Jesus were dangerous people who talked a load of rubbish. But then he heard Jesus talk to him. This changed his life. He travelled thousands of miles to tell people about Jesus.

Paul was put in jail, chained to the wall during an earthquake, shipwrecked and arrested. But he still spoke out about Jesus. Those who didn't like what he was saying thought the only way to silence him was to kill him. He was probably killed in Rome. Paul wrote lots of letters to Christians. You can read some of them in the Bible, like the letter to the Romans and one to a young Christian called Timothy.

Followers of Jesus started meeting together in groups, all over the place. They are the churches today (and we're not talking about a building!).

1 Calendars and diaries are really important to us. If we got the date wrong, we might miss the end of the school holidays and stay off school too long... (although that might not be such a disaster!)

2 But imagine missing birthdays and Christmas... (now that would be a disaster!)

3 Within 300 years of Jesus' birth, Christians, (followers of Jesus) had gone to live all over the Gulf area, much of Europe and parts of Africa. Jesus was having a real influence on the lives of many thousands of people.

4 But there was confusion about dates. In different parts of the world, people would arrive at places in the wrong month or even the wrong year!

5 So a monk called Dionysius decided, in 525 AD, to sort out the confusion and base all dates from the year of Jesus' birth. That is still the dating system used in most parts of the world! *

6 (It's worth noting that Dionysius probably got it wrong by four or five years!) But all years are now AD which is Latin for 'Anno Domini' and means 'In the year of our Lord (Jesus)'.

7 And dates before Jesus was born are known as BC, meaning 'Before Christ'. So...the year 2000 AD, marks 2000 years after Jesus was born.

*(In some parts of the world BCE (Before the Common Era) and CE (Common Era) are used instead of BC and AD.)

We might think we have a hard time... going to school, tidying our bedroom or walking the dog. But really we've got it so easy! There were times when people who believed in Jesus had it really bad!

Arguments broke out in 330 AD between Christians in Eastern Europe and those in Italy and the Gulf area. It was all over how to worship God and what to believe. Some Christians were still being put to death for saying what they believed. A number of greedy, money-grabbing church leaders were cheating ordinary people out of money and land.

In 1095, the Christian armies in Europe decided to attack the people of another religion who were living in the land where Jesus had lived. Most Christians would now say this was a dreadful thing to do. During four crusades, thousands of people on both sides were killed in battle... what a waste of life!

But despite all the unfairness, the battles, the confusion, the trouble and the arguments, the Christian Church just grew and grew and grew (like in the make-believe story of Jack's beanstalk)!

Seeing a page of words in a different language can look as though the cat has danced on the computer keyboard! If we can't understand the words, we can feel left out, as if they contain a secret that we're not allowed to know.

By 1400, most prayers and hymns were still in the ancient language of Latin. Ordinary people couldn't read them. They needed someone to tell them what it meant. There were just a few Bibles produced in English. They were handwritten. But 200 years later, Caxton made an astonishing invention. He invented machines to print books. Bibles could now be produced in large numbers. (By the way, Caxton was one of the six people nominated by the BBC as a personality of the Millennium!).

In 1525 William Tyndale became the 'father of the English Bible' when his English New Testament was published. He was arrested, strangled and burnt one year later. Then in 1611 King James allowed a version of the whole Bible to be printed and used in churches and homes. Prayers and other Christian books were also printed in English. At last some people could read the Bible for themselves and really understand it. It was like being let into a secret! As more people read the Bible, more people believed in Jesus and told others about him.

It is now very easy to find a Bible in English and one which can be easily understood by all people, including children. Parts or the whole Bible have been translated into 2211 other languages as well! To find out more, look up the last page of this book.

Over the last 200 years, people who believe in Jesus have been out to change the world! Jesus wanted sick people to be cared for, poor people to be helped and children to be loved. Christians have tried and still do try - to put Jesus' words into action. Here are some examples.

William Wilberforce hated slaves being shipped around the world. He worked to end the slave trade.

Mother Theresa saw the desperate needs of children living on the streets in India. She set up an amazing organisation to help these children.

Reproduced by kind permission of Mary Evans Picture Library.

Christians have often led the way to get rid of child labour, improve housing, and care for people, with organisations like CAFOD, Christian Aid and TEAR Fund.

Church buildings are all very different. Some are cheerful, busy places, others are pretty dull! Some are big, some are small. Some are very old, some are very modern. Many Christians meet in a home, a school or a community hall, not in a church building. And all Christians stand as signs pointing to heaven, remembering that baby born in a cowshed 2000 years ago.

2,000 years ago Jesus was born. 33 years later, he died. 3 days after that, he came back to life with a new sort of body. That means he's still alive today. He has had an amazing impact on the world. Christians believe that we can know him today.

So, that's what the Millennium is all about - don't miss it!

 All these short stories and poems have been chosen because they were written by people who have been influenced by the life of Jesus. To find out the end of each story, you will have to get hold of a copy of the book each story comes from, either in a book shop or in a library.

The Lion, the Witch and the Wardrobe
by C S Lewis.

The four children found themselves in the land beyond the wardrobe, Narnia.

"Sh! Look!" said Susan.

"What?" said Peter.

"There's something moving among the trees over there to the left."

They all stared as hard as they could, and no one felt very comfortable.

"There it goes again," said Susan presently.

"I saw it that time too," said Peter. "It's still there. It's just gone behind that big tree."

"What is it?" asked Lucy, trying very hard not to

sound nervous.

"Whatever it is," said Peter, "it's dodging us. It's something that doesn't want to be seen."

"Let's go home," said Susan. And then, though nobody said it out loud, everyone suddenly realized the same fact that Edmund had whispered to Peter at the end of the last chapter. They were lost.

"What's it like?" said Lucy.

"It's – it's a kind of animal," said Susan; and then, "Look! Look! Quick! There it is."

They all saw it this time, a whiskered furry face which had looked out at them from behind a tree. But this time it didn't immediately draw back. Instead, the animal put its paw against its mouth just as humans put their fingers on their lips when they are signalling to you to be quiet. Then it disappeared again. The children all stood holding their breath.

A moment later the stranger came out from behind the tree, glanced all round as if it were afraid someone was watching, said "Hush", made signs to them to join it in the thicker bit of wood where it was standing, and then once more disappeared.

"I know what it is," said Peter, "it's a beaver. I saw the tail."

"It wants us to go to it," said Susan, "and it is warning us not to make a noise."

"I know," said Peter. "The question is, are we to go t

it or not? What do you think, Lu?"

"I think it's a nice beaver," said Lucy.

"Yes, but how do we know?" said Edmund.

"Shan't we have to risk it?" said Susan. "I mean, it's no good just standing here and I feel I want some more dinner."

At this moment the Beaver again popped its head out from behind the tree and beckoned earnestly to them.

"Come on," said Peter, "let's give it a try. All keep close together. We ought to be a match for one beaver if it turns out to be an enemy."

So the children all got close together and walked up to the tree and in behind it, and there, sure enough, they found the Beaver; but it still drew back, saying to them in a hoarse throaty whisper, "Further in, come further in. Right in here. We're not safe in the open!" Only when it had led them into a dark spot where four trees grew so close together that their boughs met and the brown earth and pine needles could be seen underfoot because no snow had been able to fall there, did it begin to talk to them.

"Are you the Sons of Adam and the Daughters of Eve?" it said.

"We're some of them," said Peter.

"S-s-s-sh!" said the Beaver, "not so loud please. We're not safe even here."

"Why, who are you afraid of?" said Peter. "There's no one here but ourselves."

"There are the trees," said the Beaver. "They're always listening. Most of them are on our side, but there are trees that would betray us to her; you know who I mean," and it nodded its head several times.

"If it comes to talking about sides," said Edmund, "how do we know you're a friend?"

"Not meaning to be rude, Mr Beaver," added Peter, "but you see, we're strangers."

"Quite right, quite right," said the Beaver. "Here is my token." With these words it held up to them a little white object. They all looked at it in surprise, till suddenly Lucy said, "Oh, of course. It's my handkerchief – the one I gave to poor Mr Tumnus."

"That's right," said the Beaver. "Poor fellow, he got wind of the arrest before it actually happened and handed this over to me. He said that if anything happened to him I must meet you here and take you on to –" Here the Beaver's voice sank into silence and it gave one or two very mysterious nods. Then signalling to the children to stand as close around it as they possibly could, so that their faces were actually tickled by its whiskers, it added in a low whisper –

"They say Aslan is on the move – perhaps has already landed."

And now a very curious thing happened. None of the children knew who Aslan was any more than you do; but at the moment the Beaver had spoken these words everyone felt quite different. Perhaps it has sometimes happened to you in a dream that someone says something which you don't understand but in the dream it feels as if it had some enormous meaning – either a terrifying one which turns the whole dream into a nightmare or else a lovely meaning too lovely to put into words, which makes the dream so beautiful that you remember it all your life and are always wishing you could get into that dream again. It was like that now. At the name of Aslan each one of the children felt something jump in its inside. Edmund felt a sensation of mysterious horror. Peter felt suddenly brave and adventurous. Susan felt as if some delicious smell or some delightful strain of music had just floated by her. And Lucy got the feeling you have when you wake up in the morning and realize that it is the beginning of the holidays or the beginning of summer...

"And now," said Lucy, "do please tell us what's happened to Mr Tumnus."

"Ah, that's bad," said Mr Beaver, shaking his head. "That's a very, very bad business. There's no doubt he was taken off by the police. I got that from a bird who saw it done."

"But where's he been taken to?" asked Lucy.

"Well, they were heading northwards when they were last seen and we all know what that means."

"No, we don't," said Susan. Mr Beaver shook his

head in a very gloomy fashion.

"I'm afraid it means they were taking him to her House," he said.

"But what'll they do to him, Mr Beaver?" gasped Lucy.

"Well," said Mr Beaver, "you can't exactly say for sure. But there's not many taken in there that ever comes out again. Statues. All full of statues they say it is – in the courtyard and up the stairs and in the hall. People she's turned" – (he paused and shuddered) "turned into stone."

"But, Mr Beaver," said Lucy, "can't we – I mean we must do something to save him. It's too dreadful and it's all on my account."

"I don't doubt you'd save him if you could, dearie," said Mrs Beaver, "but you've no chance of getting into that House against her will and ever coming out alive."

"Couldn't we have some stratagem?" said Peter. "I mean couldn't we dress up as something, or pretend to be – oh pedlars or anything – or watch till she was gone out – or – oh, hang it all, there must be some way. This Faun saved my sister at his own risk, Mr Beaver. We can't just leave him to be – to be – to have that done to him.'

"It's no good, Son of Adam," said Mr Beaver, "no good your trying, of all people. But now that Aslan is on the move –"

"Oh, yes! Tell us about Aslan!" said several voices at once; for once again that strange feeling – like the first signs of spring, like good news, had come over them.

"Who is Aslan?" asked Susan.

"Aslan?" said Mr Beaver. "Why, don't you know? He's the King. He's the Lord of the whole wood, but not often here, you understand. Never in my time or my father's time. But the word has reached us that he has come back. He is in Narnia at this moment. He'll settle the White Queen all right. It is he, not you, that will save Mr Tumnus."

"She won't turn him into stone too?" said Edmund.

"Lord love you, Son of Adam, what a simple thing to say!" answered Mr Beaver with a great laugh. "Turn him into stone? If she can stand on her two feet and look him in the face it'll be the most she can do and more than I expect of her. No, no. He'll put all to rights as it says in an old rhyme in these parts:

> *Wrong will be right, when Aslan comes in sight,*
> *At the sound of his roar, sorrows will be no more,*
> *When he bares his teeth, winter meets its death,*
> *And when he shakes his mane, we shall have spring again.*

You'll understand when you see him."

"But shall we see him?" asked Susan.

"Why, Daughter of Eve, that's what I brought you here for. I'm to lead you where you shall meet him," said Mr Beaver.

"Is — is he a man?" asked Lucy.

"Aslan a man!" said Mr Beaver sternly. "Certainly not. I tell you he is the King of the wood and the son of the great Emperor-beyond-the-Sea. Don't you know who is the King of Beasts? Aslan is a lion — the Lion, the great Lion."

"Ooh!" said Susan, "I'd thought he was a man. Is he — quite safe? I shall feel rather nervous about meeting a lion."

"That you will, dearie, and no mistake," said Mrs Beaver; "if there's anyone who can appear before Aslan without their knees knocking, they're either braver than most or else just silly."

"Then he isn't safe?" said Lucy.

"Safe?" said Mr Beaver; "don't you hear what Mrs Beaver tells you? Who said anything about safe? 'Course he isn't safe. But he's good. He's the King, I tell you."

"I'm longing to see him," said Peter, "even if I do feel frightened when it comes to the point."

"That's right, Son of Adam," said Mr Beaver, bringing his paw down on the table with a crash that made all the cups and saucers rattle. "And so you shall. Word has been sent that you are to meet him, tomorrow if you can, at the Stone Table."

From chapters seven and eight of **The Lion, the Witch and the Wardrobe** by C S Lewis. © C.S. Lewis Pte. Ltd. 1950. Extract reprinted by permission.

The Last Enemy by Stewart Henderson

Writers have found many ways of describing what it would be like to meet God. Here Stewart Henderson writes about what it will be like at the end of time.

And he who each day
reveals a new masterpiece of sky
and whose joy
can be seen in the eyelash of a child
who when he hears of our smug indifference
can whisper an ocean into lashing fury
and talk tigers into padding roars
This my God
whose breath is in the wings of eagles
whose power is etched in the crags of mountains
It is he whom I will meet
And in whose Presence I will find tulips and
clouds
kneeling martyrs and trees
the whole vast praising of this endless creation
and he will grant the uniqueness
that eluded me
in my earthly bartering with Satan

That day when he will erase the painful gasps of
my ego
and I will sink my face into the wonder of this
glorylove
and I will watch as planets converse with sparrows
On that day
when death is finally dead.

A Wrinkle in Time by Madeleine L'Engle

*Charles Wallace goes searching for his lost father through 'a
wrinkle in time' with his sister, Meg, and friend, Calvin. They find
themselves on an evil planet, where all life is ruled by a huge,
pulsating brain known as IT. And Charles Wallace falls under the
power of IT.*

Immediately Meg was swept into darkness, into
nothingness, and then into the icy devouring cold of the
Black Thing. Mrs Which won't let it get me, she thought
over and over while the cold of the Black Thing seemed to
crunch at her bones.

Then they were through it, and she was standing
breathlessly on her feet on the same hill on which they had
first landed on Camazotz. She was cold and a little numb,
but no worse than she had often been in the winter in the
country when she had spent an afternoon skating on the
pond. She was completely alone. Her heart began to
pound.

Then, seeming to echo from all around her, came
Mrs Which's unforgettable voice. "I hhave nnot ggivenn
yyou mmyy ggifftt. Yyou hhave ssomethinngg thatt ITT
hhass nnott. Thiss ssomethinngg iss yyourr onlly
wweapponn. Bbutt yyou mmusstt ffinndd itt fforr
yyoursselllff." Then the voice ceased, and Meg knew that
she was alone.

She walked slowly down the hill, her heart thumping painfully against her ribs. There below her was the same row of identical houses they had seen before, and beyond these the linear buildings of the city. She walked along the quiet street. It was dark and the street was deserted. No children playing ball or skipping rope. No mother figures at the doors. No father figures returning from work. In the same window of each house was a light, and as Meg walked down the street all the lights were extinguished simultaneously. Was it because of her presence, or was it simply that it was time for lights out?

She felt numb, beyond rage or disappointment or even fear. She put one foot ahead of the other with precise regularity, not allowing her pace to lag. She was not thinking; she was not planning; she was simply walking slowly but steadily towards the city and the domed building where IT lay.

Now she approached the outlying buildings of the city. In each of them was a vertical line of light, but it was a dim, eerie light, not the warm light of stairways in cities at home. And there were no isolated brightly lit windows where someone was working late, or an office was being cleaned. Out of each building came one man, perhaps a watchman, and each man started walking the width of the building. They appeared not to see her. At any rate they paid no attention to her whatsoever, and she went on past them.

What have I got that IT hasn't got? she thought suddenly. What have I possibly got?

Now she was walking by the tallest of the business buildings. More dim vertical lines of light. The walls glowed slightly to give a faint illumination to the streets. CENTRAL Central Intelligence was ahead of her. Was the man with red eyes still sitting there? Or was he allowed to go to bed? But this was not where she must go, though the man with red eyes seemed the kind old gentleman he claimed to be when compared with IT. But he was no longer of any consequence in the search for Charles Wallace. She must go directly to IT.

IT isn't used to being resisted. Father said that's how he managed, and how Calvin and I managed as long as we did. Father saved me then. There's nobody here to save me now. I have to do it myself. I have to resist IT by myself. Is that what I have that IT hasn't got? No, I'm sure IT can resist. IT just isn't used to having other people resist.

CENTRAL Central Intelligence with its huge rectangle blocked the end of the square. She turned to walk round it, and almost imperceptibly her steps slowed. It was not far to the great dome which housed IT.

I'm going to Charles Wallace. That's what's important. That's what I have to think of. I wish I could feel numb again the way I did at first. Suppose IT has him somewhere else? Suppose he isn't there?

I have to go there first, anyhow. That's the only way I

can find out.

Her steps got slower and slower as she passed the great bronzed doors, the huge slabs of the CENTRAL Central Intelligence Building, as she finally saw ahead of her the strange, light, pulsing dome of IT.

Father said it was all right for me to be afraid. He said to go ahead and be afraid. And Mrs Who said I don't understand what she said but I think it was meant to make me not hate being only me, and me being the way I am. And Mrs Whatsit said to remember that she loves me. That's what I have to think about. Not about being afraid. Or not as smart as IT. Mrs Whatsit loves me. That's quite something, to be loved by someone like Mrs Whatsit.

She was there.

No matter how slowly her feet had taken her at the end, they had taken her there.

Directly ahead of her was the circular building, its walls glowing with violet flame, its silvery roof pulsing with a light that seemed to Meg to be insane. Again she could feel the light, neither warm nor cold, but reaching out to touch her, pulling her towards IT.

There was a sudden sucking, and she was within.

It was as though the wind had been knocked out of her. She gasped for breath, for breath in her own rhythm, not the permeating pulsing of IT. She could feel the inexorable beat within her body, controlling her heart, her lungs.

But not herself. Not Meg. It did not quite have her.

She blinked her eyes rapidly and against the rhythm until the redness before them cleared and she could see. There was the brain, there was IT, lying pulsing and quivering on the dais, soft and exposed and nauseating. Charles Wallace was crouched beside IT, his eyes still slowly twirling, his jaw still slack, as she had seen him before, with a tic in his forehead reiterating the revolting rhythm of IT.

As she saw him it was again as though she had been punched in the stomach, for she had to realize afresh that she was seeing Charles, and yet it was not Charles at all. Where was Charles Wallace, her own beloved Charles Wallace?

What is it I have got that IT hasn't got?

"You have nothing that IT hasn't got," Charles Wallace said coldly. "How nice to have you back, dear sister. We have been waiting for you. We knew that Mrs Whatsit would send you. She is our friend, you know."

For an appalling moment Meg believed, and in that moment she felt her brain being gathered up into IT.

"No!" she screamed at the top of her lungs. "No! You lie!"

For a moment she was free from IT's clutches again. As long as I can stay angry enough IT can't get me. Is that what I have that IT doesn't have?

"Nonsense," Charles Wallace said, "You have nothing

that IT doesn't have."

"You're lying," she replied, and she felt only anger towards this boy who was not Charles Wallace at all.

No, it was not anger, it was loathing; it was hatred, sheer and unadulterated, and as she became lost in hatred she also began to be lost in IT. The red miasma swam before her eyes; her stomach churned in IT's rhythm. Her body trembled with the strength of her hatred and the strength of IT.

With the last vestige of consciousness she jerked her mind and body. Hate was nothing that IT didn't have. IT knew all about hate.

"You are lying about that, and you were lying about Mrs Whatsit!" she screamed.

"Mrs Whatsit hates you," Charles Wallace said.

And that was where IT made IT's fatal mistake, for as Meg said, automatically, "Mrs Whatsit loves me; that's what she told me, that she loves me," suddenly she knew.

She knew!

Love.

That was what she had that IT did not have.

She had Mrs Whatsit's love, and her father's, and her mother's, and the real Charles Wallace's love, and the twins', and Aunt Beast's.

And she had her love for them.

But how could she use it? What was she meant to do?

If she could give love to IT perhaps it would shrivel

up and die, for she was sure that IT could not withstand love. But she, in all her weakness and foolishness and baseness and nothingness, was incapable of loving IT. Perhaps it was not too much to ask of her, but she could not do it.

But she could love Charles Wallace.

She could stand there and she could love Charles Wallace.

Her own Charles Wallace, the real Charles Wallace, the child for whom she had come back to Camazotz, to IT, the baby who was so much more than she was, and who was yet so utterly vulnerable.

She could love Charles Wallace.

Charles. Charles, I love you. My baby brother who always takes care of me. Come back to me, Charles Wallace, come away from IT, come back, come home.

I love you, Charles. Oh, Charles Wallace, I love you.

Tears were streaming down her cheeks, but she was unaware of them.

Now she was even able to look at him, at this animated thing that was not her own Charles Wallace at all. She was able to look and love.

I love you. Charles Wallace, I love you. I love you. I love you.

Slowly his mouth closed. Slowly his eyes stopped their twirling. The tic in the forehead ceased its revolting twitch. Slowly he advanced towards her.

"I love you!" she cried. "I love you, Charles! I love you!"

Then suddenly he was running, pelting, he was in her arms, he was shrieking with sobs. "Meg! Meg! Meg!"

"I love you, Charles!" she cried again, her sobs almost as loud as his, her tears mingling with his. "I love you! I love you! I love you!"

A whirl of darkness. An icy cold blast. An angry, resentful howl that seemed to tear through her. Darkness again. Through the darkness to save her came a sense of Mrs Whatsit's presence, so that she knew she could not be in IT's clutches.

And then the feel of the earth beneath her, of something in her arms, and she was rolling over on the sweet smelling autumnal earth, and Charles Wallace was crying out, "Meg! Oh, Meg!"

Now she was hugging him close to her, and his little arms were clasped tightly about her neck. "Meg, you saved me! You saved me!" he said over and over.

pp204–211 from **A Wrinkle in Time** © Madeleine L'Engle, Puffin 1967. Reproduced by permission of Penguin Books Ltd.

The story of the wicked tenants

Everyone, however old or young, loves a good story.
People two thousand years ago were no exception. They
would travel a long way to listen to a good storyteller.
No wonder then that Jesus, one of the greatest
storytellers ever to have lived, could hold a crowd for
hours and hours! Here's one of his stories.

A man once planted a vineyard and let it. Then
he left the country for a long time. When it was
time to harvest the crop, he sent a servant to ask
the tenants for his share of the grapes. But they
beat up the servant and sent him away without
anything. So the owner sent another servant. The
tenants also beat him up. They insulted him
terribly and sent him away without a thing. The
owner sent a third servant. He was also beaten
up terribly and thrown out of the vineyard.

　　The owner then said to himself, "What am I
going to do? I know what. I'll send my son, the
one I love so much. They will surely respect him!"

　　When the tenants saw the owner's son, they

said to one another, "Some day he will own the vineyard. Let's kill him! Then we can have it all to ourselves." So they threw him out of the vineyard and killed him.

Jesus asked, "What do you think the owner of the vineyard will do? He will come and kill those tenants and let someone else have his vineyard."

When the people heard this, they said, "This must never happen!"

But it did. The enemies of Jesus, knew he was telling this story about himself. God had sent messengers to show his people how to live the best way possible. But people ignored these messengers. So at last God sent his only son, Jesus. (That was 2000 years ago.) Surely, they will listen to him! But no, not long after Jesus told this story, his enemies arranged for him to be arrested and killed.

You can read this story in the Bible (in Luke 20: 9-16).

I am David by Anne Holm

David, who is twelve, has no memories of life before he went to live in a concentration camp in Russia. His only friend there was an older man, Johannes. He is helped to escape and so begins a dangerous journey. He has to learn to play, to be a free person and find out who he really is. He spends some time with a kind family in Italy. Then crossing the Swiss Alps, winter sets in and he finds himself working for a cruel farmer, high up in the mountains.

That winter was the longest David had ever experienced.

The farmer was an evil-hearted man. David had escaped from the wind and the snow only to be a prisoner in this man's house. It was the stable-door he had struck his head against, and that stable became his shelter for the winter – and not very good shelter either. All day long he had to work and slave as hard as he could, and a bit harder if possible. The farmer was just like one of them. He used threats to force David to work, and said he would hand him over to the police if he did not obey.

David had now learned how the members of a family spoke to one another, pleasantly and smilingly. There was nothing like that here. The farmer was cold and brutal even to his wife and two children, but David could not feel any particular sympathy for them, for the wife was a clumsy, silent woman with a sharp edge to her tongue, and as for the children – David had never thought it possible for anyone who was still a child to be so evil.

The boy was the younger, and he looked just like his father. He had stiff, straw-coloured hair and very pale blue eyes, and when he played he either destroyed something or got into mischief. He was cruel to the animals, though he knew he would get a hiding if he were found out – not that the farmer had anything against violence as such, but the animals were worth money and so they must not be ill-treated. Yet the boy could not keep his hands off them: his greatest pleasure was causing pain to a living creature.

Johannes had once said that violence and cruelty were just a stupid person's way of making himself felt, because it was easier to use your hands to strike a blow than to use your brain to find a logical and just solution to a problem.

Nevertheless it made David feel sick to see the boy's cruelty. And the girl was not much better. True, she was not cruel to the beasts, but she was not kind either. When David considered that she was about the same age as Maria, he was shocked at the difference between them. Maria with her ready smile, full of affection that she lavished on everyone, grown-ups, children, animals – even on a runaway boy... and then this girl who did nothing to please anyone – not even her own mother!

They all treated David like a dog. They threw his food to him and called him names. But they did not lay hands on him. They left him lying in the stable until he had recovered, and then they put him to work. But when during one of the first days he spent there the farmer had been about to strike him, his wife had told him to let the boy be. She had said, "You're always so stupid, Hans! He can work — I'll not meddle with that — and the stable's good enough for him. A young thief like him knows which side his bread's buttered and he'll not make a fuss about that. But if you lay hands on him, he'll murder us all in our beds. You can tell by the look of him! And the youngsters'd do well to keep out of his way if they don't want to get beaten up, that you may be sure of! You've got free labour for the winter, and that'll have to do. Then we can hand him over to the police in the spring."

David thought they were all stupid — evil, but stupid as well. If they had touched him, he would have been forced to go out into the snow again and freeze to death, but he would never have used physical violence against them. He hated them, and he would rather have let himself be killed than be like them.

In a way it was amusing. Yes, 'amusing' was the right word. Apart from hitting him, they intended to see to it that life was made as wretched for him as they could make it, and yet it was still to his advantage!

He knew now that he could never have lasted through the winter tramping the roads. He would have died of hunger and cold. At least he had shelter here, and food every day.

The stable was cold, and sometimes the snow was blown into drifts until it lay as high as the roof outside. But as it hardened, the stable grew warmer inside, and the animals added a little to the warmth.

He was not given much food, only dry bread or cold scraps, yet he had more to eat than in the camp, and it tasted no worse – sometimes, in fact, a little better.

They thought they were making him suffer by leaving him to sleep alone in the dark stable, but night was his pleasantest time!

David was not afraid of the dark. There were only common everyday objects about him, and the animals asleep. It seemed quite natural: the darkness altered nothing. What he was afraid of was people.

At night-time the stable was his. In the camp he had never been alone, and David liked to be left by himself to think in peace.

Then the dog came.

David had always thought of dogs as enemies – their tools. It was one of their pastimes to make the dogs bite the prisoners. Since his escape into Italy he had of course noticed that good people kept dogs too, but he had always given them a wide berth, just in case.

But shut up in the stable, he could not avoid the dog. It came one night when it was snowing hard and a gale was howling outside. David lay quite still and much against his will let it sniff all round him. The farmer and his family spoke a peculiar kind of German: perhaps that was the reason David spoke to it in Italian.

"I'm afraid of you," he said softly in as steady a voice as he could muster. "You're sure to notice I come from the camp, and then you'll bite me. And there's nothing I can do about it." David could see the dog as it went on sniffing round him like a big black shadow against the darkness. Then it lay down by his side, pushing and turning until they were lying back to back. It yawned very loudly, then it gave a sigh and fell asleep.

It did not bite him, and David was not nearly so cold in the night, for the dog was big and kept him warm. It was called King.

It often growled at the farmer's children, and David knew it was not very fond of the farmer, either, though he rarely struck it, no doubt because it was a good sheep-dog, and in the summer when the animals went out to graze he could not do without it.

But whenever the dog saw David, it would wag its tail, and it went to sleep with him every night.

David gradually began to grow fond of it. One evening as he lay awake wondering if the winter would ever come to an end, he held his hand out to the dog when it came to lie down beside him. He did it without thinking. Perhaps he had missed it and wanted it to come and share its warmth with him. He found himself touching its head, feeling the roundness of its skull under his hand and liking the firm warm feel of it. The dog did not move, and David let his hand glide slowly over the dog's thick coat, just once.

Then he took his hand away and lay still again.

The dog lifted its head and turned towards him and David felt its warm wet tongue carefully licking his hand.

And so David and the dog became friends.

pp 160–164 from **I am David** by Anne Holm.
English translation © 1965 Egmont Children's Books Ltd, published by Methuen & Co. Ltd. and used with permission of Egmont Children's Books Ltd.
Anne Holm is a Danish writer.

All We Need by Steve Turner

Food in our bellies
Hats on our heads
Water to quench us
Sheets on our beds.

Teachers to teach us
Shoes on our feet
Trousers and T-shirts
Shelter and heat.

Someone to love us
Someone to love
Hope for the future
Light from above.
© Steve Turner

From **The Day I Fell Down the Toilet** (Lion 1996)
© Steve Turner. Reproduced by permission of Lion
Publishing plc. Steve Turner is a poet and writer who often
shares his poetry in schools.

Secret Friends by Elizabeth Laird

She was the very first person I met on my very first day at
Dale Road Secondary School. We bumped into each other
at the door of the hall where we'd been sent to wait for our
class teachers.

"Oh, sorry," she said.

"Me too," I said.

She was much taller than me, and quite thin. She had
a bush of brown frizzy hair and pale brown skin which was
dotted all over with freckles. But what you noticed straight
away was her ears. They were large, and stuck out away
from her head. Like bat's ears.

"My name's Lucy," I said.

"I'm Rafaella," she said.

I don't know what got into me. Perhaps it was the
nervousness of starting a new school. Perhaps it was the
way she looked down at me, a little aloof, as if I was an
interesting insect miles below her.

"I can't call you that," I said, bursting into loud
laughter. "I'm going to call you Earwig. Eerie-Eerie-
Earwig."

She flushed up to the roots of her hair and turned
away.

I could tell that tears had sprouted behind her
eyelids, but she wasn't going to let me see them.

"Sorry," I said awkwardly. "Rafaella's a nice name

actually. Sort of unusual, but so what?"

It was too late. Other people, standing silently near by, not yet knowing how to talk to each other, had overheard us.

I saw one boy nudge another and look up at Rafaella's closed pale face.

"Earwig," he whispered, and they both giggled.

I've often thought I could have stopped it then and there, stood up for her, got things back on to the right track, but I didn't. I just waited, standing and fiddling with the pleats of my new navy uniform skirt, letting the laughs and the sideways glances go on round the hall.

I'm going to regret that moment till the day I die.

It's crazy, starting at a new school. For days you feel so new and lost. It's as if you've wandered into a foreign country where you can't speak the language. Then, all of a sudden, everything falls into place and you feel you've been there for ever.

The people fall into place too. It doesn't take long to work out who's going to be popular and who's going to be out of it, who's going to get into trouble and who's going to be a teacher's pet.

It was obvious, from that very first day, that Rafaella was going to be an outsider, on the edge of everything, not liked. No one actually hurt her or even teased her much. They just ignored her and left her out of things.

"What do you want, Earwig?" a group of girls would say, as Rafaella approached them.

They would stop their conversation to turn and look at her coldly, and she would blush, as she always did, mumble "Nothing," and turn away.

I was in those groups sometimes, trying to talk to Kate and Sophie, the two super-popular girls in the class. And I'd watch Rafaella and think, Not like that, you idiot. Smile. Say something cool. Don't show you care.

But after school it was different. Rafaella's house was quite near mine and we both had to get off at the same bus stop and walk down the same long road. For the first three weeks of term, we walked one behind the other and neither of us showed by a word or a look that we knew the other was there.

Then, one afternoon, she suddenly ran up behind me and said, very quickly, "Come round to my house for tea."

And I was so taken by surprise that I said, "Yes."

I regretted it at once, of course, and I started talking in a stiff, short way so as not to appear too friendly while she led me down a side road towards a small old house behind a high wooden fence. She didn't seem to notice that I was being so distant. She was as excited as a puppy who's just unearthed a bone.

I felt even more uncomfortable when she opened the front door and I followed her inside.

The house was unlike any I'd been in before.

Strange, beautiful pictures hung on the walls and old rugs covered the floors. From the front room I could hear the sound of sad foreign music and I smelled spicy food.

I wanted to turn and go home at once, but Rafaella said, "Come in here," and pushed me into the front room.

Although it was sunny outside, the curtains were half drawn. A red shaded table lamp was on, and by its light I saw nothing but books. They were stacked on shelves up to the ceiling, balanced on the old piano, piled up on the floor.

Then I saw the man. He had a white beard and was sitting in the window, a rug over his knees, his glasses slipping down over his nose. He must have been eighty years old at least.

"So," he said, and I could tell at once that he was foreign. "Rafaella has brought home a friend."

He smiled and stretched out a long thin hand, so I had to cross the room and go up to him and shake it, though I didn't want to.

"Her name's Lucy, Dad," said Rafaella.

The old man's hand was surprisingly firm and strong.

"You think I'm too old to be the father of this little girl?" he said, smiling at me, and reading my thoughts so accurately that I blushed.

"No, no, of course not," I stammered, and in fact, now that he was looking up at me, I could see that he had

Rafaella's deep set eyes, though his were pale blue, not brown, and that the ears under his bushy white hair were huge.

"Look," he said, as if he was carrying on a conversation that had been interrupted.

"This picture, so beautiful, so extraordinary, you think so?"

He pointed at the open book on his lap, and I looked down and saw whirling suns and flaming clouds, horsemen trailing banners and tigers leaping.

I wanted to look at it more closely, but Rafaella said, "She's come for tea, Dad, not for pictures," and he shut the book obediently.

"Biscuits and buns, better than art, no?"

And he winked at me.

I laughed.

He's really nice, I thought, but I couldn't imagine him being a dad. There's no chance my dad would sit looking at a book filled with pictures in the middle of the afternoon, or at any other time of the day, come to think of it.

"Darling! Here you are!"

A little woman, dark skinned and with black frizzy hair, had come into the room. "How was the torture chamber today?"

She hadn't seen me.

Rafaella pulled me forward.

"This is Lucy, Mum," she said. "I've brought her home for tea."

"How wonderful! How lovely!"

Rafaella's mother seemed extraordinarily pleased, as if I was a princess or something. She smiled with her whole face, patting my arm with her soft hand.

She looked as young as my mum, but different in every other way. Her clothes were foreign and so was her voice, though not in the same way as her husband's. She might have been from some southern or eastern country. I couldn't tell.

"How lucky," she said, with a chuckle that came from deep in her throat. "I made sweets today."

We had tea in the kitchen, sitting round the little table, nibbling at strange things made of honey and nuts. I'd never seen things like that before. I tried one, but I wasn't sure of it and I didn't want any more, so Rafaella fetched out a packet of biscuits and I ate a lot of those.

The three of them kept pouring more tea into my cup and smiling at me and asking me questions as if I was a strange being from outer space, as if I was the first outsider who had ever walked into their house.

"Oh! Your mother!" said Rafaella's mother suddenly. "She'll be worried so much that you haven't come home!"

"No she won't," I said. "She doesn't finish her shift till six."

I left at last, full of tea and biscuits, feeling good.

Rafaella and her mum waved to me as I walked away, standing with their arms round each other's waists.

They really love each other, I thought enviously. They like being with each other. They're really nice.

From **Secret Friends** by Elizabeth Laird. Reproduced by kind permission of Hodder and Stoughton Limited.

Elizabeth has written many books for children. She's won the Smarties Young Judges Award (where all the judges are children) for her book, **Kiss the Dust**.

The tree climber's surprise

Jesus always had time for the people who were left on the outside - the disabled, the poor, cheats and those from ethnic minority groups. Here is the story of the time when he gave one little cheat the biggest surprise of his life.

Jesus was going through Jericho, where a man named Zacchaeus lived. He was in charge of collecting taxes and was very rich. Jesus was heading his way, and Zacchaeus wanted to see what he was like. But Zacchaeus was a short man and could not see over the crowd. So he ran ahead and climbed up into a sycamore tree.

When Jesus got there, he looked up and said, "Zacchaeus, hurry down! I want to stay with you today." Zacchaeus hurried down and gladly welcomed Jesus.

Everyone who saw this started grumbling, "This man Zacchaeus is a sinner! And Jesus is going home to eat with him."

Later that day Zacchaeus stood up and said

to the Lord, "I will give half of my property to the poor. And I will now pay back four times as much to everyone I have cheated."

Jesus said to Zacchaeus, "Today you and your family have been saved, because you are a true son of Abraham. The Son of Man came to look for and save people who are lost."

You can read this story for yourself in the Bible (in Luke 19:1-10).

Basil in Blunderland by Basil Hume

Basil Hume who died in June 1999, was the Roman Catholic Archbishop of Westminster. He was one of the best-known leaders of the church in the UK. On his death, the Chief Rabbi, Jonathan Sacks said, "Cardinal Hume was a man of God who turned strangers into friends."

Basil in Blunderland – an odd title for a book, no doubt, and maybe one to surprise. Let me explain. A long time ago – well, nearly twenty years ago – I used to give talks to young people who came from time to time to Archbishop's House. Sometimes sixty or more would come. Many were teenagers, some were bright, some even brighter. None would claim to be learned. They came for some theology. That gave the whole thing respectability. We used to call those evenings 'theology for the eleven minus'…

When we came together we used to discuss important matters about God and ourselves, but in a simple manner. We did not go in for learned footnotes or long words, or thoughts that were too abstract. The talks were simple, solid and, unless I am badly mistaken, interesting too. Exploring God and his world together is interesting, and, indeed, enjoyable too.

Then an enjoyable event in my life occurred. On holiday in Scotland, with a family I knew well, I found myself one day being invited by the junior members of the family to play hide-and-seek. There was no problem about that in principle. But on this occasion there was a snag. As a monk I was required to do half an hour's mental prayer each day. That day, when invited to play hide-and-seek, I had not, in fact, meditated. So I had a problem. How does one play hide-and-seek and, at the same time, meditate? Trying to solve that very considerable problem became the subject of my talks to the 'eleven minus'. The hiding places suggested thoughts about the spiritual life. ...

So you are invited to join the members of that lovely group who listened to earlier versions of these talks. They were patient and understanding. I trust that you, the reader, will be also.

Now to the game. Kate and Barney are getting impatient.

The Larder

We had to decide who was going off to hide first. The choice was Barney. Kate and I turned round and faced the wall and started to count up to twenty, very slowly, of course. Barney shot off as quickly as he could. I would like to remind you that when playing hide-and-seek, once you have found the person then you let out a great shout of triumph. That is the end of that round. But the game we were playing was slightly different. Once one of us had found the person hiding, the two of us would stay together until the third had succeeded in discovering us. It is a special kind of hide-and-seek.

I found Barney first. He was in a room which is generally next to the kitchen. It is a very important room. It is called the larder. Larders used to be even more important when there weren't any of those modern things like fridges and freezers. How on earth did we manage without a fridge? Sometimes there was a kind of detached extension to the larder. This was often in the back-yard. It had a funny door with lots of holes in it so that air could get in and the cat could not. But you couldn't hide here. The entrance was too small. But this is all slightly by the way. The larder proper was where you had sacks of potatoes on the floor and dishes of yesterday's food on the shelves. Its entry was from the kitchen. Barney was hiding in the larder. Kate had gone off in a different direction, so I had plenty of time to continue my meditation. I started to think about the larder. I remembered something that I was told when I was a very small boy. This is the story.

In a larder there was a stack of apples. Nobody knew exactly how many. A small boy wanted an apple. He had been told by some grown-up that he must not take things from the larder without permission. Taking things without permission that belong to other people was called 'stealing'. But, as I have said, nobody knew how many apples there were and, in any case, the small boy was all alone in the larder. Why not take one? Nobody would know. It just seemed common sense. He was hungry and wanted an apple. Why should he not have one? Nobody would see him. Was that true? Nobody? One person would. That was God. He sees everything you do, and then punishes you for the wrongdoing, so I was told.

It took me many, many years to recover from that story. Deep in my subconscious was the idea of God as somebody who was always watching us just to see if we were doing anything wrong. He was an authority figure, like a teacher or a policeman or even a bishop.

Now, many years later I have an idea that God would have said to the small boy, "Take two". I must explain that God never encourages us to steal. I have to make this rather obvious and ponderous statement because someone – no doubt learned and very good – once wrote to me to explain that God doesn't want us to steal. Of course not. So please do not go round to your neighbourhood green grocer and take two apples!

The point of my story is to explain that God is not the kind of person who is watching you all the time to catch you out. He is on our side unless we walk away from him deliberately. If our idea of God is of a stern authority figure, then we shall always be a little bit twisted. Fear will be dominant in our relationship with God. We have to think of him, not as an authority figure, but as a loving father.

One day I told this story on radio. It later appeared in a parish magazine. A lady wrote to me and said: I read your story about the larder. It reminded me of something told to me by an aunt. She went on to describe how in the aunt's house there was one of those funny old notices in flowery writing. It was a passage from scripture. The text was: "Thou God seest me". But the lady said, "Yes, God is always watching you. Because he loves you so much he cannot take his eyes off you."

That is a wonderful thought. God can't take his eyes off me. Wherever I am and whatever I am doing, he keeps on looking at me, not to catch me out, but from love...

Eventually Kate arrived. I had to bring my meditation to a close. I was now prepared for the next round of hide-and-seek. I felt so much happier now because once again I had reflected on the great love which God has for me. And I decided I didn't want to do anything wrong because I didn't want to displease one who loved me so much and trusted me so greatly. Who goes off to hide now?

From **Basil in Blunderland** by Cardinal Basil Hume, 1997. Reproduced by kind permission of Darton, Longman & Todd Ltd.

The Journey of the Magi by TS Eliot

TS Eliot wrote many plays and poems. Just imagine what it was like to be one of the wise men (Magi) travelling to meet the child, Jesus, at the very first Christmas.

'A cold coming we had of it,
Just the worst time of the year
For a journey, and such a long journey:
The ways deep and the weather sharp,
The very dead of winter.'
And the camels galled, sore-footed, refractory,
Lying down in the melting snow.
There were times we regretted
The summer palaces on slopes, the terraces,
And the silken girls bringing sherbet.
Then the camel men cursing and grumbling
And running away, and wanting their liquor and women,
And the night-fires going out, and the lack of shelters,
And the cities hostile and the towns unfriendly
And the villages dirty and charging high prices:
A hard time we had of it.
At the end we preferred to travel all night,
Sleeping in snatches,
With the voices singing in our ears, saying
That this was all folly.
Then at dawn we came down to a temperate valley,

Wet, below the snow line, smelling of vegetation,
With a running stream and a water-mill beating the
darkness,
And three trees on the low sky.
And an old white horse galloped away in the meadow.
Then we came to a tavern with vine-leaves over the lintel,
Six hands at an open door dicing for pieces of silver,
And feet kicking the empty wine-skins.
But there was no information, and so we continued
And arrived at evening, not a moment too soon
Finding the place; it was (you may say) satisfactory.

All this was a long time ago, I remember,
And I would do it again, but set down
This set down
This; were we led all that way for
Birth or Death? There was a Birth, certainly,
We had evidence and no doubt. I had seen birth and death,
But had thought they were different; this Birth was
Hard and bitter agony for us, like Death, our death.
We returned to our places, these Kingdoms,
But no longer at ease here, in the old dispensation,
With an alien people clutching their gods.
I should be glad of another death.

T S Eliot (1888-1965) from **Ariel Poems**, Faber & Faber
1927 (US Harcourt Brace) Reproduced with permission.

The Christmas Mystery by Jostein Gaarder

. . . perhaps the clock hands had become so tired of going in the same direction year after year that they had suddenly begun to go the opposite way instead . . .

Dusk was falling. The lights were on in the Christmas streets, thick snowflakes were dancing between the lamps. The streets were crowded with people.

Among all these busy persons were Papa and Joachim, who had gone into town to buy an Advent calendar. It was their last chance, because tomorrow would be the first of December. They were sold out at the news stand and in the big bookstore at the market.

Joachim tugged his father's hand hard and pointed at a tiny shop window where a brightly coloured Advent calendar was leaning against a pile of books.

"There!" he said.

Papa turned back. "Saved!"

They went into a little bookshop that Joachim thought looked old and worn out. Books stood tightly packed on shelves along all the walls from floor to ceiling, all of them different. A large pile of Advent calendars lay on the counter. There were two kinds, one with a picture of Santa Claus with a sled and a reindeer and the other with a picture of a barn with a tiny little elf eating porridge out of a big bowl.

Papa held up the two calendars.

"There are plastic figures in this one and chocolate ones in that," he said, "but the dentist won't be too happy about that."

Joachim examined the two calendars. He didn't know which one he wanted.

"It was different when I was a boy," continued Papa.

"How do you mean?"

"Then there was only a tiny picture behind each door, one for each day. But it was exciting every morning, trying to guess what the picture would be. Then we opened it… well, we opened it, you see. It was like opening the door to a different world."

Joachim had noticed something. He pointed to one of the walls of books. "There's an Advent calendar over there too."

He ran over to fetch it and held it up to show Papa. It had a picture of Joseph and Mary bending over the baby Jesus in the manger. The three Wise Men from the East were kneeling in the background. Outside the stable were the shepherds with their sheep and angels floating down from the sky. One of them was blowing a trumpet.

The colours of the calendar were faded as if it had been lying in the sun all summer, but the picture was so beautiful that Joachim almost felt sorry for it.

"I want this one," he said.

Papa smiled. "You know, I don't think this one's for

sale. I think it must be very old. Maybe as old as I am."

Joachim wouldn't give up. "None of the doors are open."

"But it's only here on display."

"I want it," repeated Joachim. "I only want one that's like none of the others."

The bookseller came up – a man with white hair. He looked surprised when he saw the Advent calendar.

"Beautiful!" he exclaimed. "And genuine – yes, original. It almost looks home-made."

"He wants to buy it," explained Papa, pointing at Joachim. "I'm trying to explain that it's not for sale."

The man raised his eyebrows.

"Did you find it here? I haven't seen one like that for years."

"It was in front of all the books," said Joachim.

"Oh, it must be old John up to his tricks again," said the bookseller.

Papa stared at the man. "John?"

"Yes, he's a strange character. He sells roses in the market, but where he gets them from, nobody knows. Sometimes he comes in and asks for a glass of water. In summer when it's hot he'll pour the last drops over his head before he goes out again. He's poured a few drops over me a couple of times, too. To thank me for the water he sometimes leaves one or two roses on the counter; or he'll put an old book on the bookshelf. Once he put a photograph of a young woman in the window. It was from a country far away – maybe that's where he comes from himself. 'Elisabet', it said on the photo."

"And now he's left an Advent calendar?"

"Yes, evidently."

"There's something written on it," said Joachim. He read aloud: "MAGIC ADVENT CALENDAR. Price 75 øre."

The bookseller nodded. "In that case it must be very old."

"May I buy it for 75 øre?" asked Joachim.

The man laughed. "I think you should have it for nothing. You'll see, old John had you in mind."

"Thank you, thank you, thank you," replied Joachim, on his way out of the bookshop already.

Papa shook the bookseller's hand and followed Joachim out on to the pavement.

Joachim hugged the calendar tight. "I'll open it tomorrow," he said.

Joachim kept waking up that night, thinking about the bookseller and John with his roses. Once he went to the bathroom and drank water from the tap, and thought of John pouring water over his head. Most of all he thought about the magic Advent calendar. It was as old as Papa, but all the same, nobody had opened any of the doors.

Before he went to bed he had found all the doors from 1 to 24. The twenty-fourth was of course Christmas

Eve, and that door was four times bigger than the others, covering almost the whole of the manger in the stable.

Where had the magic Advent Calendar been for over forty years? And what would happen when he opened the first door?

When he woke up again and it was seven o'clock, he reached up for the calendar, which was hanging above his bed, to open the first door. His fingers were so impatient and nervous that it was difficult to get hold of it properly. At last he managed to loosen a tiny corner, and the door opened slowly.

Joachim gazed into a picture of a toyshop. Among all the toys and the people were a little lamb and a small girl, but he couldn't look at the picture in detail, for just as he opened the door something fell out on to his bed. He bent down and picked it up.

It was a thin sheet of paper, folded over and over. When he had smoothed it out he saw that there was writing on both sides. So he read what was on the paper.

THE LAMBKIN

"Elisabet!" her mother called after her. "Come back, Elisabet!"

Elisabet Hansen had been standing staring at the big pile of teddy bears and furry animals while her mother was buying Christmas presents for the cousins who lived at Toten. All of a sudden a little lamb shot out of the pile. It jumped on to the floor and looked around. It had a bell round its neck, and the bell started to jingle in competition with all the cash registers.

How could a toy suddenly come to life? Elisabet was so surprised that she started to chase the lamb. It was running across the wide floor of the department store in the direction of the moving staircase.

"Lambkin, lambkin!" she called after it.

The lamb was already on the staircase, which was moving down to the floor below. The stairs moved quite quickly, and the lamb sprang even quicker, so that Elisabet had to run faster than the stairs and the lamb together if she was going to catch up with it.

"Come back, Elisabet!" repeated her mother severely.

But Elisabet had already jumped on to the staircase. She could see the lamb running through the ground floor where they sold underwear and ties.

As soon as she had solid ground beneath her feet again, she went the same way as the lamb. It had managed to bound out on to the street where the snowflakes were dancing among the chains of Christmas lights hanging above the street. Elisabet knocked over a stand of winter gloves and followed it.

Out in the noisy street she could barely hear the bell jingling. But Elisabet did not give up. She was determined to stroke the lamb's soft fleece.

"Lambkin, lambkin!"

The lamb sprang across the road against a red light. Perhaps it thought a red man meant "Go!" and a green man meant "Stop!". Elisabet thought she had heard that all sheep were colour blind. At any rate, the lamb didn't stop, so Elisabet couldn't stop either. She was going to catch up with the lamb even if she had to follow it to the ends of the earth.

The cars tooted their horns, and a motorbike had to swerve on to the pavement to avoid colliding with Elisabet or the lamb. The people doing their Christmas shopping all stared. They didn't often see a little girl running across the road after a lamb. In any case, it was strange to be running after a lamb in the middle of winter.

As they ran, Elisabet heard the church clock striking three. She noticed it specially, because she knew she had come to town on the five o'clock bus. Perhaps the hands had become so tired of going in the same direction year after year that they had suddenly begun to go the opposite way instead. Elisabet thought that clocks, too, might get bored with doing the same thing all the time.

But there was something else as well. When Elisabet had gone into the department store, it had been almost completely dark. Now it was suddenly light again, and that was curious, because there had been no night in between.

As soon as the lamb had a chance, it found a road leading out of town, and trotted on towards a small wood.

It sprang on to a path between tall pine trees. Now the lamb had to slow down a little, for the path was covered with all the snow that had been falling during the past few days.

Elisabet went after it. It was difficult for her to run now, too. But the lamb had four legs which were dragging in the snow, while she had only two. Perhaps that would help her to gain on it.

Her mother's cries had been drowned long ago by the noise in the street. Soon she couldn't even hear the street sounds. But something was still singing in her ears:

"Shall we buy this one, or both of them? What do you think, Elisabet?"

Perhaps the reason the lamb had come to life and run away from the big store was that it could no longer bear to listen to the cash registers and the talk about buying and selling. And perhaps that was why Elisabet was following it. She never enjoyed shopping.

Joachim looked up from the sheet of paper that had fallen out of the magic Advent calendar. What he had read was so amazing.

He had always liked secrets. Now he remembered the little box with the key in it, the one Grandma had bought him in Poland. Mama and Papa had made him a solemn promise that they would never look for the key and open the box when Joachim was asleep or at school. It would have been as bad as opening someone else's letters, they had said.

Up to now Joachim hadn't had any real secrets to hide in the box, but now he put the paper from the Advent calendar there, turned the key, and hid it under his pillow...

For the rest of the day Joachim wondered whether Elisabet would catch up with the lamb so that she could stroke its fleece. Would he find out tomorrow?

For then there'd surely be another little piece of paper?

... I know of a short cut, and that's the path we're taking now...

Joachim woke up before Mama and Papa the next morning too, but then he nearly always did. He sat up and looked at the Advent calendar. Only now did he notice a little lamb lying at the feet of one of the shepherds. Wasn't that strange? He had spent a long time looking at the picture with all the angels and the Wise Men, the shepherds and their sheep, but he had never noticed the lamb.

Perhaps it was because he had read about the lamb on the piece of paper that had fallen out of the calendar. But that lamb had jumped out of a modern shop – and the lamb on the Advent calendar had lived in Bethlehem, long ago. There were no cars and traffic lights then, and no big stores with escalators and cash registers. Besides, Elisabet had heard the church clock striking three, and surely there were no church clocks two thousand years ago? Joachim knew that that was when the baby Jesus was born.

Now he found the door with a number 2 on it, and opened it carefully. A folded piece of paper fell out of the calendar as the door slowly opened. He peeped in at a picture of a wood, where an angel stood with his arm round a little girl.

Joachim bent down and picked up the scrap of paper that had fallen into the bed. He unfolded it and saw that something was written on it in tiny letters on both sides of the page. And he began to read.

EPHIRIEL

Elisabet Hansen didn't know how far nor how long she had run after the lamb, but when she set off through the town it had been snowing heavily. Now it had not only stopped snowing, there was no snow on the path either. Among the trees she could see blue anemones, coltsfoot and windflowers, and that was unusual, because it was very nearly Christmas.

She picked up an anemone and looked at the blue petals carefully. Picking flowers at this time of year was every bit as mysterious as throwing snowballs at Midsummer.

It occurred to Elisabet that perhaps she had run so

far that she reached a country where it was summer all year round. If not, she must have run for so long that spring and the warm weather had arrived already. In that case, she might still be in Norway, but then, what would have happened to Christmas?

While she stood wondering she heard the tinkle of a bell in the distance. Elisabet started running again and soon caught sight of the lamb. It had found a small grassy bank and was grazing on it greedily. The little creature had probably been very hungry. It had not had any grass to eat as long as it was winter. It had certainly not had a morsel of food as long as it had been a toy either, and that may have been for a very long time.

Elisabet crept up towards the lamb, but just as she was about to pounce on it in order to stroke it, it sprang away again.

"Lambkin, lambkin!"

Elisabet tried to keep up with it, but she tripped over a pine root and fell flat on the ground.

The worst of it was that she realised she was unlikely ever to catch up with the lamb. She had decided to follow it to the ends of the earth, but the earth was round, after all, so they might go on running round the world for ever, or at any rate until she grew up, and by then she might have lost interest in such things as lambs.

When she looked up she caught sight of a shining figure between the trees. Elisabet looked, wide-eyed, for it was neither an animal nor a human being. A pair of wings were sticking out of a robe as white as the lamb.

Elisabet had only just managed to get to know the world. She had learned what all the commonest animals were called, but she didn't know the difference between a tomtit and a yellowhammer. Nor between a camel and a dromedary, come to think of it. All the same, there was no mistaking what she was looking at now. Elisabet realised at once that the shining figure must be an angel. She had seen angels in books and pictures but it was the first time she had seen one in real life.

"Fear not!" said the angel in a gentle voice.

Elisabet raised herself halfway up.

"You needn't think I'm afraid of you," she replied, a little sulkily because she had fallen and hurt herself.

The angel came closer. It looked as if he was hovering just above the ground. It reminded Elisabet of her cousin Anna who could dance on the tips of her toes. The angel knelt down and stroked her gently on the nape of her neck with the tip of one of his wings.

"I said, 'Fear not', to be on the safe side," he said. "We don't appear to humans very often, so it's best to be careful when we do. Usually people are frightened when they're visited by an angel."

Suddenly Elisabet began to cry, not because she was afraid of angels, and not because she had hurt herself either. She didn't understand why she was crying until she heard herself sob, "I wanted . . . to stroke the lamb."

The angel nodded gracefully. "I'm sure God wouldn't have created the lambs with such soft fleece unless he hoped someone would want to stroke it."

"The lamb runs much faster than I do," sobbed Elisabet, again, "and it has twice as many legs too. Isn't that unfair? I can't see why a little lambkin should be in such a hurry."

The angel helped her to her feet and said confidentially, "It's going to Bethlehem."

Elisabet had stopped crying. "To Bethlehem?"

"Yes. To Bethlehem, to Bethlehem! For that's where Jesus was born."

Elisabet was very surprised at what the angel said. In an attempt to hide her astonishment she began to brush soil and grass off her trousers. There were some nasty stains on her red jacket too.

"Then I want to go to Bethlehem," she said.

The angel was dancing on the tips of his toes again on the path.

"That suits me," he said, hovering above the ground. "I'm going there too. So we might just as well keep each other company, all three of us."

Elisabet had learned that she should never go anywhere with people she didn't know. That certainly applied to angels as well. So she looked up at the angel and asked, "What's your name?"

Elisabet had thought that the angel was a man, but she wasn't quite sure. Now he curtseyed like a ballet dancer and said, "My name is Ephiriel."

"That sounds like a butterfly. Did you really say Ephiriel?"

"Just Ephiriel, yes. Angels have no mother or father, so we have no family name either."

Elisabet sniffed for the last time. Then she said, "I don't think we have time to talk any more if we're going all the way to Bethlehem. Isn't it a long way?"

"Yes indeed, it's very far – and a very long time ago. But I know of a short cut, and that's the path we're taking now."…

THE TWENTY-FOURTH OF DECEMBER

…a spark from the great beacon behind those weak lanterns in the sky…

Christmas Eve began as usual. There was always some last-minute task that had to be done, and last-minute presents to be wrapped up. Now and again one of them would sneak into Joachim's room and glance expectantly at the magic Advent calendar. They had promised not to open it until the bells rang Christmas in.

Later in the day they began to prepare Christmas dinner. Before long the whole house was smelling of Christmas. At last it was five o'clock. Papa opened a window, and now they could hear the church bells ringing.

Nobody said anything, but they all crept into the bedroom. Joachim climbed on to the bed and opened the last, big door in the calendar. It was the one that covered the manger with the Christ-child. The picture beneath it showed a cave in a mountain.

For the last time they sat on the edge of the bed. Joachim unfolded the thin sheet of paper and read aloud to Mama and Papa.

THE CHRIST-CHILD

It's the middle of the world between Europe, Asia and Africa. It's in the middle of history at the beginning of our era. Soon it will be the middle of the night as well.

A silent crowd is stealing upwards between the houses in Bethlehem. They are a little flock of seven sheep, four shepherds, five angels of the Lord, three Kings of Orient, one Roman Emperor, the Governor of Syria, and Elisabet from the long, narrow country below the North Pole.

The weak glow of oil lamps is streaming from the windows in a few of the simple houses, but most people in the old town have gone to bed for the night.

One of the Wise Men points up at the sky where the stars are burning in the darkness. They are like sparks from a beacon far away. One star is shining more brightly than all the other stars in the sky. It looks as if it's hanging a little lower in the sky as well.

"O little town of Bethlehem.
How still we see thee lie.
Above thy deep and dreamless sleep
The silent stars go by,"
murmurs Elisabet softly, remembering an old carol.

The angel Impuriel turns towards the others, puts a finger to his lips, and whispers, "Hush... Hush..."

The procession of pilgrims gathers in front of one of the inns of the town. In a moment or two the innkeeper appears at the window. When he sees the group outside he nods firmly and points to a cave in the wall of rock.

The angel Ephiriel whispers something; it sounds like the words of a nursery rhyme.

'And while they were there, the time came for her child to be born, and she gave birth to her son, her first-born. She wrapped him in swaddling clothes, and laid him in a manger, because there was no room for them in the inn.'

They creep across the yard and stop in front of the cave. The smell from it tells them that it is a stable.

Suddenly the silence is broken by the cry of a child.

It is happening now. It is happening in a stable in Bethlehem.

Over the stable a star is twinkling. Inside the stable the new-born child is wrapped in swaddling clothes and laid in a manger.

This is a meeting of heaven and earth. For the child

in the manger is also a spark from the great beacon behind those weak lanterns in the sky.

This is the wonder. It is a wonder every time a new child comes into the world. This is how it is when the world is created anew under heaven.

A woman is breathing deeply and weeping. Not out of sadness. Mary is weeping quietly, deeply and happily. But the child's cries drown out Mary. The Christ-child is born. He has been born in a stable in Bethlehem. He has come to our miserable world.

The angel Ephiriel turns solemnly towards the other pilgrims and says,

'Unto you is born this day in the city of David a Saviour.'

The Emperor Augustus nods.

"And now it's our turn. Everyone is to take up their places, everyone must remember their lines. We have rehearsed this for almost two thousand years."

Quirinius speaks, at a sign from the Emperor.

"Shepherds! Take your flock out into the fields, and never forget to be Good Shepherds. Wise Men! Depart to the desert and mount your camels, each one of you. May you never cease to read the stars in the sky. Angels! Fly high above the clouds, all of you. Do not reveal yourselves to people on earth unless it is absolutely necessary, and never forget to say, 'Fear not!' For now Jesus is born."

The next moment all the shepherds and sheep, the

angels and the Wise Men, had vanished. Elisabet was left alone with Quirinius and the Emperor Augustus.

"I must hurry home to Damascus," said Quirinius. "I have an important role to play there."

"And I must go back to Rome," said Augustus. "That is my role."

Before they went, Elisabet pointed at the stable and asked, "Do you think I may go in?"

The Emperor smiled from ear to ear.

"Of course you are to go in. That is your role."

Quirinius nodded energetically.

"You haven't come all this long way just to hang about."

With those words the two Romans started running back along the way they had come.

Elisabet looked up at the starry sky. She had to tilt her head far back to see the big star which was shining so brightly. Again she heard the cry of a child from inside the cave.

So she went into the stable.

pp 2–13, 166–168 from **The Christmas Mystery** by Jostein Gaarder, Reproduced by kind permission of Phoenix House Publishers.

My Dad by Steve Turner

My dad's better than your dad.
My dad's as tall as the moon,
as strong as the wind,
as wide as the sky.
You should see my dad!
He's got stars in his fists.
He bends rainbows on his knee.
When he breathes, clouds move.

He's good is my dad.
You can't scare him with the dark.
You can't scare him with guns or sticks.
He makes bullies say sorry
just by staring.
Big green monsters
fall asleep in his lap.
Ghosts start haunting each other.

My dad's been everywhere
but he says he likes the world.
Earth people are fun he says.

My dad knows more than teacher.
He knows everything.
He knows what you're thinking,
even when you try to trick him
by thinking something else.
If you tell a lie
my dad says he can tell
by the look on your face.

My dad's the best dad ever.
I say I love him
a million times a million
times a million times a million trillion.
My dad says he loves me
a billion trillion times more than that.

My dad likes to love.
My dad made the world.

From **The Day I Fell Down the Toilet** (Lion 1996)
© Steve Turner. Reproduced by permission of Lion
Publishing plc.

A new Millennium is about to begin. Does that make you excited or not? If you could have one wish for a child born on 1 January 2000, what would it be? We asked the people on the next few pages the following question:

What present would you give to a child born on 1 January 2000?

Some of the people are famous, some of them are not. Some are old, some are very young. How would you answer that question?

Message from Andy

"A mountain! Tall, rugged and proud", says Andy Hawthorne. "Children of the Millennium will face massive challenges. To overcome them they'll need a strong belief in an awesome God and an attitude that refuses to give in.

This baby will begin to explore the world, by playing on the grassy slopes of the mountain. 'This is my mountain - but how can I climb it?' Rumours of nasty things like wolves and bears would stop him or her from going higher. But life will become boring. This Millennium child, now a sharp young person, will want higher adventure.

It will be a struggle to climb the zig-zag path to the top. But one day, hot from the climb, the summit comes into view. Breathless but laughing, this Millennium child will look down at the valley below, then look out into the rest of life now in view. He or she will be confident that after this experience and with God, they now can tackle anything."

Andy Hawthorne is the founder of the World-wide Message Tribe and director of the Message Trust. This exists primarily to present the Christian message relevantly to teenagers in Manchester.

at present would you give to a child born on 1 January 2000?

Christmas Toddler

Samuel Boshoff was born on 23 December 1997. His dad helped him to write this:

If, like me, you have a birthday near Christmas, you spend all year waiting and waiting for presents to arrive. And then suddenly you get lots all at the same time!

I would have two presents for a baby born on 1 January 2000. First, lots of patience for all the waiting he'll have to do until the next present-time arrives. Secondly, a present that's so good he'll enjoy it for the whole year without getting bored – like a big book with lots of different stories.

Dad has a really big book with lots of stories in it. But there's one problem. It looks really boring – just millions of words in tiny writing and no pictures. Whenever I pick it up, I tear out pages by mistake and Dad gets annoyed.

But yesterday Dad gave me another book with lots of stories. This one has great pictures and is made of strong stuff so I can throw it across the room when I've finished the story for the day, and nobody seems to mind! Dad says my one is called the Bible and so is his! Lucky me to get the interesting version. The baby can have one like mine...

What present would you give to a child born on 1 January 20

All the way from Samoa

"A coconut tree from my homeland Samoa," says Apollo Perelini. "It has often been said that the Island of Samoa, where I come from, captures the beauty of the garden of Eden.

The coconut tree is bare, slender, tall and leans in the breeze. Yet in a wild storm, it stands resilient and strong. At the foot of the tree, the roots are firmly set in the ground.

The palms can be woven into baskets, mats and thatch for roofs. The coconut provides a drink, kept cool by the thickness of the husk. The fibre of the husk is very strong and is used to make rope. Beneath the husk is the hard shell. It can be used for drinking vessels and bowls. Inside the shell is the white meat. It can be eaten as it is, or a creamy milk can be squeezed from it. Then the trunk itself can be turned into building materials.

I would give a coconut tree so that this child may understand that God created things in nature to help us to live. God is a bit like the coconut tree. He provides for everything we need. We have clothes, food and shelter. When problems come, we can stand tall and strong if we root ourselves in God's ways."

Apollo Perelini has played Rugby League for St Helens since 1994. Before that he played Rugby Union in New Zealand and he played for West Samoa in the 1991 World Cup!

at present would you give to a child born on 1 January 2000?

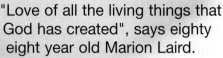

"Love of all the living things that God has created", says eighty eight year old Marion Laird. "That means plants, animals, birds and insects, as well as an appreciation of the many cultures and races in the world.

I learned my love of nature from my father. He was a doctor in a small country town in New Zealand. My husband John, was a doctor too. We were both interested in people from different backgrounds from our own. We wanted to work in China, but my husband's health wasn't good enough. Instead, he became a ship's surgeon. We sailed round Cape Horn, where icebergs floated around us in the great Southern Ocean.

John gave up being a doctor to work full-time for Scripture Union. That's an organisation that helps people, especially children, to get to know God and read about him in the Bible. After the Second World War, we moved to London. Our house was often full of people who came from all over the world. They taught us a great deal about their own cultures.

I'm old now, and I often sit at the window and look out into the garden – the changing seasons, the flowers that blossom and fade, the visiting birds and insects. They all still fill me with delight. I would wish that every child might feel that too."

What present would you give to a child born on 1 January 20

The words of a monk

"I was born just before the Second World War and lived in London during very heavy bombing," says Dom Basil, the abbot of Elmore Abbey. "I did not expect to survive. But I did, and have always regarded life as a gift.

When I became a Christian at the age of twenty-one, I went to church for the first time. I wanted to be with people who shared my faith in God and worshipped him. I wanted to learn all about him. I was twenty-six when I became a monk. Thirty-six years later, I do not regret that decision. I am still adding to my understanding of what the word 'God' means. The more you know, the more there is to know! God is so great – like the universe, but much bigger!

My present would be something that lasts, not something you can eat or gets worn-out but something to treasure and keep. I have a crucifix, (a model of the cross), to remind me of the greatest act of love, giving one's life for a friend. That's what Jesus did. It was given to me as a Confirmation present and now stands on my desk. I have treasured it for a long time. I would like to share it by handing it on to someone else.

Living in a monastery means learning to share and offer hospitality. Visitors are always made welcome."

Abbot Basil Matthews lives at Elmore Abbey, an Anglican Benedictine Monastery.

at present would you give to a child born on 1 January 2000?

A teenager on New Year's Eve

Louisa Willoughby was born at 8.30pm on New Year's Eve, 1986. That means she'll become a teenager just three and a half hours before the year 2000 begins.

"What really annoys me is when people don't accept others for who they are. I'm 50% deaf in both ears and for most people that's not a problem. They just accept me as I am. Then there are the wars which happen because one group of people refuses to accept another group, like in Kosovo. Lots of people don't accept who they are. They pretend to be someone else.

I would give this baby the ability to love and accept people for who they are – and to love and accept themselves too!"

Time for young people

"My present is not something that you can find in the local toy store. It's time!" says Ishbel Munro working in Enniskillen among young people.

"Being a youthworker, I know how important it is to children and young people to spend time with them. It may mean going out for a coffee, or in the case of a baby, playing with them for an afternoon. It means not being so busy that you don't have time to listen. Time is not something to be bought. It's more precious than the most expensive gift!"

Ishbel Munro works for Careforce in Enniskillen in Northern Ireland

What present would you give to a child born on 1 January 20

Sally

Sally Magnusson is a journalist and broadcaster. She lives with her five children near Glasgow.

"A baby born on 1 January 2000 will be so weighed down with meaningful presents that I'd like to give her something she might actually find useful straightaway. A dummy. I agree this is not a very exciting gift, but it will at least give her something to do that day while her mum and dad are stuffing themselves with the New Year roast lunch and celebrating the arrival of the new Millennium.

It will be a comfortable companion for the next few years. When she gets to the age of two, she can start firing it out of her mouth like a bullet when anyone she doesn't like comes into the room.

Unfortunately it's usually considered a good idea to get rid of the dummy before starting school, which is not fair, I know, but don't worry. She can get it mounted on the wall and keep it for ever to remind her of the first day of the new century, the day she was born."

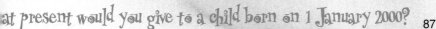

at present would you give to a child born on 1 January 2000?

Film-making for children

Derek Butler is the Commissioning Executive for BBC Education

"I've spent thirty years making films. For the last ten of these, the films, on many subjects and for all ages, have been shown on BBC2 television. You may have seen some of them – Watch, Storytime and Science Zone. The thrill of making these programmes is to take some important idea and make it fun, interesting and easy to understand. My favourite subjects are Science and Religious Education. Many adults will say these were the two subjects they found either difficult or boring – sometimes both. Let me let you into a secret. Sometimes the reason for this was that they had a bad teacher.

So what I would give this child is a voucher that would give them the right to be taught by the best science and RE teachers in the country. Then they'd realise how brilliant both are and also learn another simple lesson very clearly: that both subjects are trying to understand the world we all grow up in by asking different questions. Science is asking 'how'? And religion is asking 'why'?"

What present would you give to a child born on 1 January 20

The Toybox Charity

Rachel Potter lives 7000 miles away in Guatemala City, South America, working for The Toybox Charity, which rescues homeless children. The Toybox Charity provides homes, food, medicine and clothes for these children. Toybox also has a special school for street children – a safe place for them to eat, have a shower and learn to read and write.

"1500 street children struggle to survive on the streets of Guatemala without anyone to care for them," says Rachel Potter. "Thousands more have some kind of home but no schooling and no one to care for them properly. So I would give this baby a home because a home means so much. Home is:

- a place where the baby will be loved and cared for instead of feeling unwanted.

- a place where they can learn about God's great love for them instead of experiencing the pain of rejection.

- a place where they can grow up with good memories of fun times, laughing and playing together instead of living with constant worries and fears.

- a place where they can have a shower and clean clothes every day instead of feeling dirty, smelly and hungry.

- a place where they would have an opportunity to go to school and study, to learn to do something useful with their life instead of feeling hopeless.

- a place where they would have their own warm bed and someone to say "goodnight" instead of a cold pavement and no one to care."

What present would you give to a child born on 1 January 2000?

"I live in a large house in Folkestone with my parents and Granny. I have two brothers and one sister. We have lots of foreign visitors at our house and I like talking to them and having supper with them. I have two dogs and a cat, fish and stick insects so our house is very busy. My school has a farm with animals like pigs, chickens, sheep, cows and rabbits and we grow plants, flowers and vegetables.

I go to St. John's Church. I sing bass in the music group. Every Sunday I go to U-Turn for teenagers. I play football, listen to talks about the Bible, talk to friends and pray to God and sing. I like church. I am a scout, and I like swimming, badminton, cricket and golf.

My present would be the gift of music. I would play my cornet for the baby and I would make soft music when it was going to sleep. I would play pop music, which is jumpy, to make it happy, and loud music to make the baby clap to the beat. The baby could learn to dance to music. Animal noises and unusual noises would make the baby laugh.

I think music would be a lovely present because it would be always changing and would cheer the baby up if it was sad or lonely."

John will be 17 on 17 December 1999.

What present would you give to a child born on 1 January 200

Joker and thinker

Twin brothers, Christopher and Patrick Neilands live in Belfast, Northern Ireland. They may look alike but their characters are different. Christopher is the joker, who usually takes charge. Patrick is more of a thinker.

One of the best things about being twins, they say, is always having someone to thump. One of the worst things is having to share a bedroom and clothes.

Something Christopher and Patrick don't mind sharing is friends. They have plenty of schoolmates, but their very best friend is their next-door neighbour Ruairi, who's eight. The boys hold regular meetings in the garden shed. They call themselves the Fab Four (Ruari's older sister used to be a member, but these days she's too busy with homework and Irish dancing). They have a club project to save endangered species. So far they've raised 50p!

As his gift for the Millennium baby, Christopher would give a peaceful mind. "Hating makes you do things that give other kids a bad feeling inside," he says. "I'd give the child the sort of mind that doesn't want to kill or hate."

Patrick says his gift would be a world full of friendship. "I'd like the child to grow up in a world where people and animals are friends and where God and people are friends. I'd especially like the child to have a best friend like Ruairi living next door."

at present would you give to a child born on 1 January 2000?

Professor!

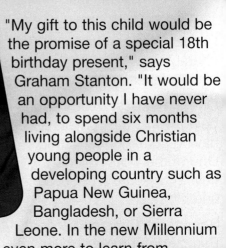

"My gift to this child would be the promise of a special 18th birthday present," says Graham Stanton. "It would be an opportunity I have never had, to spend six months living alongside Christian young people in a developing country such as Papua New Guinea, Bangladesh, or Sierra Leone. In the new Millennium we will have even more to learn from Christians in such countries than we do at present. They will be able to teach us that following the way of Jesus Christ brings joy and inner peace even though in 2018 they are still unlikely to have many of the possessions we take for granted in western countries. I hope that by this date western countries will have learned to share the earth's resources more fully and more fairly with all people in the world God has created.

Although I have been privileged to travel in many countries of the world, and to teach some very able students from developing countries, I have never had the opportunity to live in a non-western country. I was brought up in New Zealand, before travelling to Cambridge for advanced study of the New Testament. I have been privileged to teach, study, and write about the New Testament for 28 years – and I still have plenty to learn!"

Graham Stanton is the Lady Margaret's Professor of Divinity in the University of Cambridge.

What present would you give to a child born on 1 January 20

Dear Baby

Dear Baby

My name is Eilidh Cameron. I'm 8 years old and I have a black pet rabbit called Sooty. My bedroom is full of toy rabbits because they're my favourite animal. I have a younger brother called Calum. I love reading, swimming and playing games with my seven friends.

I would give a baby born on 1 January 2000, a great big hug so it knew how special it was to me and Jesus, and a soft toy rabbit to cuddle when I'm not there.

Love Eilidh (*Eilidh lives in Edinburgh.*)

Meet Horace

Dawn Clancy and her cheeky friend Horace live and work in Plymouth. They visit lots of schools to take assemblies. Horace is always rude to the teachers and Dawn tells Bible stories and paints pictures. They visit each school about twice a year and see about 20,000 children!

Dawn: Horace, how would you answer the question?

Horace: Err... it would have to be a Bible, because a Bible would tell them all about Jesus and he's the best!

Dawn: But what if they never looked at it?

Horace: Ah, I didn't think of that – we could make them!

Dawn: Don't be silly, you can't do that. I've got a better idea.

Horace: You have?

Dawn: If I knew that child, I could *tell* them about Jesus! I would tell them that Jesus can be their friend too, if they ask him. Then, they can read more about him in the Bible.

Horace: That sounds a great idea, Dawn!

at present would you give to a child born on 1 January 2000?

TV Presenter

"For my present, I would book the baby on a pilgrimage to a place called Medjugoria which is a small village in the former Yugoslavia. I would have to reserve a place for the baby a few years after it was born – it is that popular! When I was about fifteen, I travelled with my school to Medjugoria. It is a wonderful place. For many years, people have travelled there – people of all ages. During their stay they have met with God in a special way. I went there with an open mind, not quite knowing what to expect. But as the week went on I soon realised that something fantastic and spiritual was happening there.

Medjugoria is very much a place to reflect on your life, a place to pray and grow close to God and for me it was a place to realise what life was really all about – something every newly-born baby should be given the chance to experience later in life.

Medjugoria is in the Herzegovina region of former Yugoslavia. It's not been touched by the civil war and has been a haven for the United Nations. It did get bombed a couple of times but amazingly the bombs didn't go off. Some people think that this was a miracle. It's remained a 'no war zone' in the middle of a 'war zone'."

Chris Rogers is a TV presenter.

What present would you give to a child born on 1 January 20

Driving a London Bus

"Hello baby, all red and wrinkly like a shrivelled-up plum!" whispers Rustom Battiwalla. "I can see that you have a lot of gurgling and dribbling to do, but I just want to give you this. I'll put him down next to you so that you can give him a cuddle – after all, that's what teddy bears are for. I know he's a very old teddy and doesn't look much, but I've had him since I was little and he's been a good friend to me.

You see, I'm a bus driver, and all day long I watch people getting on and off my bus. Many of them look so sad and serious that I wonder if they've forgotten what it's like to love and be loved. I know I shall never be rich or famous, but I'm happy because people love and care about me. That's far more important. Look after teddy for me, and don't forget to give him a hug from time to time.

Listen, I must go now. I've got a bus to catch. Bye!"

at present would you give to a child born on 1 January 2000?

Jesus is the person who has had more influence on the whole world than anyone else. After reading *Stories for the Millennium*, you may want to find out more about Jesus. Reading about him in the Bible is a good place to begin. There are four accounts of his life, written by Matthew, Mark, Luke and John. Make a start with Luke's story. You'll find that more than halfway through the Bible. Use the contents page to find out where exactly.

There are lots of Bibles you can buy. Many schools and churches use the *Good News Bible*. And if you want a booklet to help you understand what the Bible says (sometimes it can be a bit difficult!) *Snapshots* and *One Up* have been written to help you. *Snapshots* is for children aged 8-10 and *One Up* is for 11-14s. You can find them in a Christian bookshop or ring 01908 856182 for information.